Reduce, Reuse, Recycle

Helen Lanz

W
FRANKLIN WATTS
LONDON•SYDNEY

This edition 2012

First published in 2010 by
Franklin Watts
338 Euston Road
London NW1 3BH

Franklin Watts Australia
Level 17/207 Kent Street
Sydney NSW 2000

Series editor: Julia Bird
Design: D.R. ink
Artworks: Mike Phillips

A CIP catalogue record for this book is available
from the British Library.

ISBN 978 1 4451 0915 2
Dewey classification: 363.7'28

Picture credits: Monica Adamczyk/istockphoto: 16b;
Arvind Balarman/Shutterstock: 12bl; Blackbeck/istockphoto: 27b;
Jeffrey Blacker/Alamy: 23b; Bubbles/Alamy: 20t; Tony Campbell/
istockphoto: 11b; Cultura/Getty Images: 1, 26; Randy Faris/Flame/
Corbis: 17; Nick Free/istockphoto: 27t; Ben Frederick/PD: 20b; Grandpa/
Shutterstock: 12tr; David J Green/Alamy: 15b; Home Studio/
Shutterstock: 21t; Stephanie Horrocks/istockphoto: 13tr: Jupiter Images/
Alamy: front cover t; LACSD: 8; Scott Latham/Shutterstock: 11t; Magnus/
Alamy: 16t; Ian Miles/Flashpoint Pictures/Alamy: 7; David Noble
Photography/Alamy: front cover cr; Paul O'Connor/Alamy: 18bl;
Skip O'Donnell/istockphoto: 24b; Brandon Parry/Shutterstock: 19b;
Patrimonio Designs/Shutterstock: 25t; Photoalto/Alamy: 24t;
Recycle Now Partners: 19t; Reportage/Getty Images: 10;
Reuters/Corbis: 9; Christina Richards/Shutterstock: 15t;
Hughette Roe/istockphoto: 22b; Ilan Rosen/PD: 21b.
Mark Ross/Shutterstock: 18tr; Vladimir Sazonov/Shutterstock.

Printed in China

Franklin Watts is a division of Hachette Children's Books,
an Hachette UK company.
www.hachette.co.uk

*To my dad, whose jokes are largely recycled and
all a load of rubbish!*

"*During 25 years of writing about the environment for the* Guardian*, I quickly realised that education was the first step to protecting the planet on which we all depend for survival. While the warning signs are everywhere that the Earth is heating up and the climate changing, many of us have been too preoccupied with living our lives to notice what is going on in our wider environment. It seems to me that it is children who need to know what is happening: they are often more observant of what is going on around them. We need to help them to grow up respecting and preserving the natural world on which their future depends. By teaching them about the importance of water, energy and other key areas of life, we can be sure they will soon be influencing their parents' lifestyles, too. This is a series of books every child should read.*"

Paul Brown
Former environment correspondent
for the *Guardian*, environmental author
and fellow of Wolfson College,
Cambridge.

Contents

Words in **bold** can be found in the glossary on page 28.

What a waste!

What have you eaten or used today? Did you have to throw anything away? We all throw things away every day. A wrapper around something we've eaten, an apple core, a piece of paper that we've drawn on. This is our 'waste' or rubbish.

A whole load of rubbish!

Imagine this: if you live in the UK, the USA or Australia, you probably throw away seven times your weight in rubbish every year! This rubbish is likely to include three plastic bottles, four glass bottles, 13 metal cans and 5 kg of paper a week. The USA tops the charts for the country that makes the most waste, Australia comes second, and the UK throws away the most rubbish in Europe.

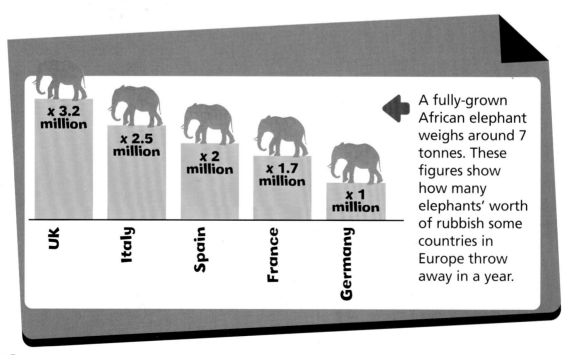

x 3.2 million — UK

x 2.5 million — Italy

x 2 million — Spain

x 1.7 million — France

x 1 million — Germany

A fully-grown African elephant weighs around 7 tonnes. These figures show how many elephants' worth of rubbish some countries in Europe throw away in a year.

In Europe, about 3,500 dustbins-full of rubbish are thrown away every minute.

Why do we make so much rubbish?

We haven't always made so much waste. Nowadays, food and other goods are much more heavily packaged than they used to be, meaning we have more **packaging** to throw away. We also tend to buy more products, such as clothes, toys and electrical goods, than people used to, and we keep them for less time before throwing them away. Most importantly, there are many more of us in the world than there used to be. The Earth's **population** has multiplied by four times in the last 100 years, and more people equals more waste.

What happens to our waste?

There are lots of ways of disposing of waste, but to get rid of most of our rubbish, we dig huge holes in the ground and bury it. This is known as **landfill**. We can also burn or **recycle** rubbish.

The Puente Hills Landfill is the biggest landfill in the USA. It can hold 13,000 tonnes of rubbish a day.

Burying the problem

In landfill sites, the waste is placed in holes, or 'cells', which are lined with plastic to stop the waste from **polluting** the soil. However, as the rubbish slowly **rots**, liquid waste and gas often do leak out. Rotting food makes a gas called **methane** which leaks into our air, while liquid waste can get into the **groundwater** and pollute our water supplies. Our rubbish takes a long time to rot – for example, a plastic bottle can take over 450 years to break down – so buried rubbish is going to be a problem for a long time.

CASE STUDY

DUMPING GROUND

While developed countries, such as the USA and UK, bury their rubbish, developing countries, such as India, often heap theirs up into massive, rotting piles. This is dangerous and extremely bad for people's health. And what's also shocking is that sometimes this rubbish is not from the people themselves, but from people in developed countries who have paid to dump their waste somewhere else.

In Mumbai, India, nearly 500,000 people live near a rubbish dump.

Going up in smoke

Waste can also be incinerated, or burned. Some countries in Europe, such as Denmark, incinerate over half their waste. The process gives off several gases, including **carbon dioxide** (CO_2), which are harmful to our environment, though many modern incinerators can use the heat from the incinerator to make electricity.

Recycling

Recycling rates vary around the world, but account for around 32% of waste disposal in the USA and UK. Rubbish is taken to a recycling plant where it is broken down so that the **material** it is made from, such as glass, paper or metal, can be used to make new products, such as bottles, newspapers and cans.

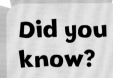

Did you know?

Up to 80 % (that's most) of what we throw away could be reused or recycled.

Resources and fossil fuels

By simply throwing things away and buying new things, we use up more and more of the Earth's **natural resources**, such as wood, water and metal. This is because the more products we make, the more resources we use to make them. We also use the Earth's **fossil fuels** to give us the power to actually make the new products.

To make just one computer and its screen uses metal, glass, **chemicals**, 240 kg of fossil fuels and 1.5 tonnes of water.

Fossil fuels

Coal, oil and natural gas are known as fossil fuels because they are formed under the ground over millions of years from the remains of plants and animals. Fossil fuels are used to generate electricity and electricity is used in factories to make new products for us to use and buy. However, our supplies of fossil fuels are running out and they cannot be replaced.

Hotting up

The Earth is surrounded by a layer of gases called the **atmosphere**. The Sun's rays can shine through this layer, but it also keeps in the Sun's heat. When we burn fossil fuels, they release carbon dioxide. This gas is good at trapping heat so, with more of it in the atmosphere, the Earth is heating up. This is known as **global warming**. As we burn more and more fossil fuels to make products, the rate of global warming is increasing.

 Carbon dioxide traps heat like the glass in a greenhouse. That's why it is also called a **greenhouse gas**.

Climate change

As the temperature of the Earth changes, it is changing our weather patterns. Extreme weather events around the world, such as floods, **drought** and violent storms, are becoming more common. This is called **climate change**.

The Earth's climate varies naturally, but floods like this are becoming more common.

Reduce your use

Luckily, there is plenty we can all do to help solve our rubbish problem. Have you heard of the 'three Rs' – reducing, reusing and recycling? Many of you probably already recycle some of your rubbish. But what about 'reducing' or 'reusing' it?

Cut down

Reducing is the first step to take in cutting down on waste. Reducing means exactly that – reducing how much waste we make in the first place.

The more we buy, the more waste we produce.

ONE EARTH OR TWO?

If all of the people on the Earth bought as much as people in the USA, we would need three to five more new Earths just to fit in all these things that have been bought, and to have enough resources to make all these things in the first place.

Our Earth is amazing, so let's use its resources carefully.

Think about it

Reducing our use is all about asking ourselves whether we really need to buy something new, or whether we can get by without it. Companies want us to buy the latest clothes, toys and electronic gadgets so they make money, but the truth is that we often lose interest in our new things quite quickly.

It is more likely for us to remember happy events from our childhood rather than the things we had.

Less is best

When you do decide to buy something, try to choose a product that has less packaging. Some packaging is needed to protect the product, but lots of flashy packaging just creates more waste. Food and drinks packaging helps to keep them fresh, but try not to buy individually wrapped items. These have lots of wasteful packaging and are more expensive than buying food and drink in bulk.

At Christmas time in the UK, 800,000 tonnes of toy packaging – that's about the same weight as 115,000 African elephants – end up in landfill.

Can't reduce? Reuse!

If you simply have to have a new toy, gadget or game, how about buying one that has already been used, or simply borrowing one for a while? This saves resources and money.

Reusing in action

We already reuse things, probably without thinking about it. Do you ever borrow books, CDs or DVDs from the library? Or play with your older brother's or sister's toys? You may even wear 'hand-me-downs' from older brothers or sisters. These are all examples of reusing things.

Pass it on

If you don't want something anymore, don't just throw it away. You could try passing it on to a friend, or there are plenty of places to take old toys, books and clothes. Charity shops, door-to-door collections and clothes collection points all take clothes and goods to sell on or give to people and countries in need.

Get online

It's now really easy to pass on or sell things online. A website called Freecycle can put you in touch with people in your local area who want to find or get rid of all sorts of things, from furniture to bicycles. If you'd like to sell your things instead, you could ask your parents to help you look at websites like Ebay.

Charity shops sell on second-hand clothes, books and DVDs to raise money for charity.

Selling your old things over the Internet can help to raise money to buy something else (second-hand, of course!).

Did you know?

The fossil fuels used to produce one computer chip weigh 600 times the weight of the chip.

Reuse again

If you want to make the best use of your things, you should also look at what you buy in the first place. Things that are well made will last and can be used again. However, if something does break, rather than throw it away, perhaps it could be repaired?

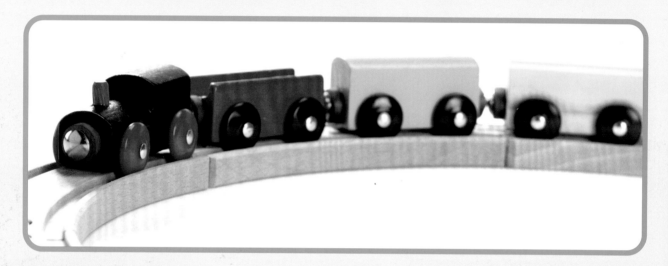

Make it last!

Try to avoid using **disposable** things whenever you can. If you take a packed lunch to school, try to avoid pre-packed snacks that create lots of rubbish. If you use plastic plates or cutlery, wash and reuse them. If you're going on holiday, try not to take a disposable camera that you can only use once.

 Well-made toys last a long time and can be passed on to brothers and sisters, and even sons and daughters.

Reuse your bags

Keep plastic bags to reuse when you go shopping. Plastic bags are bad for the environment as they take so long to break down, or biodegrade, in landfill (see page 8), so make a difference by reusing your old bags rather than taking new ones. Alternatively, take reusable cloth bags with you when you go shopping.

Reusable cloth bags are stronger than plastic bags, as well as being a lot better for the environment.

PLASTIC IS NOT SO FANTASTIC!

It is believed that in Australia, about 429,000 plastic bags end up in landfill every hour, or 7,150 bags every minute.

In 2008, 9.9 billion plastic shopping bags were given out in the UK – that's about 160 bags per person. Laid end-to-end, these would stretch to the moon and back seven times!

Recycle! Recycle! Recycle!

If you can't reuse something and it can't be repaired, perhaps the materials that it is made from could be used again? This is recycling. It saves landfill space, **energy**, money and resources, and helps to reduce pollution.

Waste paper

A lot of the rubbish in our bins is paper or cardboard waste. We use paper every day in a variety of products, from packaging to phone directories. In the UK alone, each family uses about six trees-worth of paper every year. Companies worldwide use enough paper in a day to wrap around the Earth 20 times.

 Look out for the mobius loop on goods and packaging. It shows that something can be recycled.

The wonders of wood

Wood is a **renewable** resource – trees can be planted and grown specially to be cut down and used to make paper. But recycling used paper and card saves not only trees, but also landfill space, energy and money.

The trees in this forest are specially grown to be made into paper.

How it works

It is usually easy to recycle paper and cardboard. Many homes have a kerbside service where the local council pick up waste paper that's been collected at home and take it to a recycling facility. If your local council doesn't run a kerbside collection, you can take old paper and cardboard to recycling banks in your local area.

New products

All sorts of products can be made out of recycled paper and card. Newspapers and magazines are mostly made from recycled paper, and you can buy recycled paper pads and toilet paper. But recycled paper can also be used to make a variety of other products including loft insulation, animal bedding, lampshades and even ornaments!

Many schools and businesses recycle their paper waste, too.

This colourful pot is made from recycled magazines.

Did you know?

If we recycled all our waste paper, over 250 million trees could be saved a year.

Recycling glass and plastic

Did you know that people have dug up glass that is over 3,000 years old? That tells us that glass doesn't break down very quickly! But it can be recycled over and over again without losing its quality. So don't bin that bottle – recycle it.

Dos and don'ts

There are some dos and don'ts about recycling glass. Make sure you wash any bottles or jars out, and separate them by colour at home or at the recycling bank. Don't put in any heat-resistant glass, such as Pyrex, light bulbs or non-see-through glass, as these can spoil a whole batch of glass.

 Separate your glass into green, brown or clear glass before taking it to the bottle bank.

New glass

Once it's been recycled, glass has many uses. It can be re-made into bottles or jars, made into jewellery, or mixed with other materials and used for building. It is also used to make a substance called glassphalt which is used in road surfaces.

 Glassphalt helps car tyres to grip the road surface.

BOTTLES, BOTTLES, BOTTLES

Over six billion glass bottles and jars are used in the UK every year.

The energy saved from recycling just one glass bottle will power a television for 20 minutes, a computer for 25 minutes or a 100-watt light bulb for four hours.

Plastic problem

It is thought that some plastic objects could take more than 450 years to break down. So it's scary to think that in the USA alone, over two million plastic bottles are thrown away every hour.

Plastic dos and don'ts

Plastic objects can often be recycled along with your household waste, but check first. There are lots of different types of plastic, so make sure it shows the recycling loop before you put it in the recycling bin. Also remember to 'wash and squash' before you recycle!

New plastic

Recycled plastic can be turned into new bottles, garden furniture, carpets and even clothes. It takes just 25 plastic bottles to make a fleece jacket!

Recycled plastic can be made into colourful raincoats.

Recycling metal

Did you know that your car could be made out of the same material as a food tin or a drinks can? Aluminium and steel are metals and are used to make all sorts of things, from car parts to packaging. Both metals can be recycled over and over again to make anything from bikes to bridges.

Haven't I seen you somewhere before?

Nearly 60% of aluminium used today has been recycled. So your car may well have a few old drinks cans in it!

Save energy

It takes a lot of energy to make things from fresh aluminium or steel; it saves a lot of energy to make things from recycled aluminium and steel. For example, it takes the same amount of energy to make 20 recycled aluminium cans as it does to make one new can. Yet at the moment, we only recycle a fraction of the metal that we could.

IN THE CAN

In the UK alone, over 2.5 billion cans are recycled every year, saving 125,000 tonnes of solid metal waste going to landfill.

Aluminium cans are crushed before recycling.

THE WAR EFFORT

During World War Two (1939–1945), materials were in short supply because everything was being used in the war effort. Everybody recycled everything they could. Metal straps were taken from corsets (underwear) and enough metal was saved to build two warships!

Dos and don'ts

There's plenty you can do to help. Be sure to wash out any cans before recycling. Check foil wrapping to see if it is aluminium; if it springs back to shape, it is not aluminium and cannot be recycled. How about collecting cans at school for 'Cash for Cans' centres or 'Cans and bottles for a cause' schemes to raise money for your school or good causes?

An aluminium can can be recycled, made into a new can, filled and be back on the shelf in just six weeks.

23

Recycling electronics

Many homes in developed countries are full of electronic equipment – from Playstations™ to washing machines. But what do we do with the old products when they break down or newer versions are in the shops? Most are just thrown away.

 Over 75% (or three quarters) of electrical appliances end up in landfill.

Friends might enjoy playing your old computer games.

Think about it

Before you decide to throw away your electronic game, first see whether you can give it to a friend, donate it to a local charity shop or sell it online (see page 15). If it's broken, find out whether it can be repaired.

Recycle with care

If your electronic product can't be given away or repaired, check with your local council whether they will pick it up and arrange for it to be recycled, as many offer this service. Many electronic items contain dangerous substances that would pollute the environment, so make sure that they are recycled with care.

Symbols such as these indicate that a product shouldn't go in the household bin. Most electronic goods can't go in the bin, but many can be recycled.

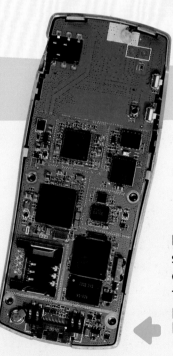

CASE STUDY

IT'S THE PHONE!

Mobile phones are built to last for about seven years, but we tend to buy new phones every 11 months or so. About 150 million mobile phones a year are thrown away in the USA – wasting enough energy to power 285,000 homes for a year. Rather than just throwing your old phone away, try giving it away or recycling it.

Precious metals, such as gold and copper, are found in mobile phones and can be reused.

Keep the loop going

There are many good reasons to reduce, reuse and recycle. It can save resources, energy, landfill space and money, and reduce pollution.

Could do better!

The good news is that most countries are recycling more each year, but many countries could still recycle a lot more material than they currently do.

In 2008, the European Parliament set waste recycling targets for all countries in the European Union. By 2020, 50% of all household waste and 70% of all building waste must be recycled. If a country fails to reach these targets, they will face stiff penalties.

 By working together, we can all help to recycle more and more of our rubbish.

Power of the people

That's all of us! If we all reduce our use, reuse and recycle, we can save enormous amounts of natural resources, energy, money, space and pollution. We all need to look at our habits – do we really need to keep buying more things? If we do need to buy, try to buy products made from recycled materials, and once you've finished with these, recycle them again. This truly completes the recycling loop.

 Help complete the loop. Recycle your waste, then buy it back as something else!

THE POWER OF RRR

Recycling just under a tonne of paper saves 17 trees, 2 barrels of oil, enough energy to power the average home for 6 months, saves enough landfill space to fit the size of a family people carrier, and saves over 27 kg of air pollution.

Our world is full of beautiful places. It is up to us to protect these places so we can continue to enjoy them in the future.

Glossary

Atmosphere The layer of air around the Earth.

Carbon dioxide A gas in the air around us.

Chemical Something that has been made through a chemical process. For example, detergents are chemicals that clean things by removing dirt particles.

Climate change Longterm changes to the Earth's weather patterns.

Developed countries Countries with well-developed economies, where most of the population work in factories and businesses.

Developing countries Countries with less-developed economies, where most of the population work in farming.

Disposable Designed to be thrown away after it has been used.

Drought A shortage of rain over a long period of time.

Energy The power to make or do something.

Fossil fuels Fuels such as coal, oil or gas, which have developed under the ground from rotting animal and plant life over millions of years.

Global warming The gradual heating up of the Earth's atmosphere.

Greenhouse gas A gas, such as carbon dioxide, that creates an invisible layer around the Earth, keeping in the heat of the Sun's rays.

Groundwater Water from rain that collects and flows under the Earth's surface.

Landfill Areas for dumping and burying household or industrial waste.

Materials What something is made from, such as cotton, wood or metal, for example.

Methane A gas produced when food or plants rot. It is also made by animals when they digest (break down) their food. Methane is a powerful greenhouse gas.

Natural resources Materials, such as water and wood, that are found in nature.

Packaging The box or wrapping that surrounds a product.

Polluting Making something, such as water or the air, dirty.

Population The number of people living in a place.

Recycle To break something down so that the materials that it is made from can be used again.

Renewable Something that is in constant supply and will not run out, such as the wind.

Rots When something, such as food, goes mouldy and starts to smell.

Useful information

Throughout this book, 'real life measurements' are used for reference. These measurements are not exact, but give a sense of just how much an amount is, or what it looks like.

African elephant = 7 tonnes

Earth's circumference at Equator = 40,000 km

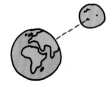

Average distance from Earth to the moon= 384,500 km

Further reading

The Green Team: Waste and Recycling by Sally Hewitt (Franklin Watts, 2011)

Re-Using and Recycling series by Ruth Thompson (Franklin Watts, 2009)

Environment Detective Investigates: Reducing and Recycling Waste by Jen Green (Wayland, 2010)

Websites

www.olliesworld.com
Tips on how we can all reduce, reuse, recycle and rethink.
www.recyclezone.org.uk
Fun recycling activities.
www.kidsrecyclingzone.com
All about recycling at home and at school.

Dates to remember

Earth Hour – 31 March

Earth Day – 22 April

World Environment Day – 5 June

Clean Air Day – June

Walk to School Campaign – May and October

World Food Day – 16 October

Buy Nothing Day – 24 November

Note to parents and teachers: Every effort has been made by the Publishers to ensure that these websites are suitable for children, that they are of the highest educational value, and that they contain no inappropriate or offensive material. However, because of the nature of the Internet, it is impossible to guarantee that the contents of these sites will not be altered. We strongly advise that Internet access is supervised by a responsible adult

Index